Buffy
The Spiritual Player

Save Yourself

BUFFY

BALBOA.PRESS
A DIVISION OF HAY HOUSE

Balboa Press books may be ordered through booksellers or by contacting:

Balboa Press
A Division of Hay House
1663 Liberty Drive
Bloomington, IN 47403
www.balboapress.com
844-682-1282

Because of the dynamic nature of the Internet, any web addresses or links contained in this book may have changed since publication and may no longer be valid. The views expressed in this work are solely those of the author and do not necessarily reflect the views of the publisher, and the publisher hereby disclaims any responsibility for them.

The author of this book does not dispense medical advice or prescribe the use of any technique as a form of treatment for physical, emotional, or medical problems without the advice of a physician, either directly or indirectly. The intent of the author is only to offer information of a general nature to help you in your quest for emotional and spiritual well-being. In the event you use any of the information in this book for yourself, which is your constitutional right, the author and the publisher assume no responsibility for your actions.

Any people depicted in stock imagery provided by Getty Images are models, and such images are being used for illustrative purposes only.
Certain stock imagery © Getty Images.

Print information available on the last page.

ISBN: 978-1-9822-5779-8 (sc)
ISBN: 978-1-9822-5781-1 (hc)
ISBN: 978-1-9822-5780-4 (e)

Library of Congress Control Number: 2020921473

Balboa Press rev. date: 02/09/2021

Contents

How It Started

In my dream at the age of eighteen, while I was trying to save this little girl's life, lying in my bed, screaming and crying for help, the girl yelled, "Save her! It's in the book!"

In real life, I woke up screaming, crying, and terrified. Having gone through hell and back, I understand now, at the age of forty-two, that I had to save myself and share my story with other people who find themselves stuck in a life filled with abandonment, rejection, manipulation, poverty, physical abuse, sexual abuse, and emotional abuse, and having nowhere to run, seeing no way out, suffering in silence. When you finish reading this book, I hope you will be able to find the wisdom and courage to turn your heart from pain to hope, faith, and pleasure.

During my years growing up, my city was labeled as one of the murder capitals of the country.

I was considered a quiet child, an observer and loner who questioned everything about life. In 1996, the day after my high school graduation, I left town. I made it out of Indiana, which was everyone's dream. I became successful without a family to support me, and I was on my own on multiple occasions with two kids. Many people have asked me, "How did you make it out, and how are you able to now live a life you love?"

It wasn't easy. After many years of watching and experiencing the histology of a loved one suffering with schizophrenia; a friend imprisoned for murder; a father who was an alcoholic, womanizer, and woman beater; a relative who became involved in gang-related activities in his youth;

poverty all around; childhood abuse; panic attacks; depression; and the pain of neglect, abandonment, molestation, and verbal and physical abuse as well, I emerged with tremendous strength.

I managed to accomplish every dream and goal I envisioned for myself. If I only knew then what I know now! I would have dreamed a little bigger, judged a lot less, focused more on what I wanted, and made decisions out of love and not fear. But I know my journey was necessary because I am here now sharing my testimony and wisdom with you.

My purpose is to share my story on how I discovered that my **thoughts were becoming things** before I knew the word *manifestation* ever existed. My desire is to speak to those individuals who may have been born and programmed in the same dimension as I have. I was completely unaware that love was my birthright. I sure as hell didn't know I was born into a false perception about my reality until the God in me awakened, after years of praying, stepping out on faith, running for peace, crying and hoping for a better life for myself and my daughters, hitting my rock bottom, and then deciding to live, after writing my suicide letter to my kids.

I discovered I was never alone—not even in the shower, in my prayer closet, or washing dishes, and especially when this African prince left me in tears on my birthday with $500 to my name, the beatings, the abuse, homelessness, betrayal, and the ugly hatred from people I love. That is when I learned I was truly created in the likeness of God. So, what does this mean for all of us? Straight to the point. We have been creating hell and heaven on Earth all this time through our beliefs. Isn't that something?

In October 2012, I was thirty-five years old, and for the first time in my life, I was able to see the synchronicity in my life called manifestation and a quantum leap. I found these terms while I was searching for answers to who I was, after manifesting an entire new life. During my research, I discovered a power I was born with that I never knew was in me. I finally understood how and why I made it out of Indiana. I understood why, no matter where I moved, who I dated, and who I married, I kept experiencing the same circumstances that caused my own suffering. I finally understood I was responsible for my own life. I knew why I kept experiencing the same stuff at work and in every other aspect of my life. I understood why people are still in the hood and killing folks like damn fools.

My awakening also answered my questions from my childhood: why do church folks struggle year after year? It didn't make any sense. I just couldn't understand why good people who praise and worship God every Sunday, pray, give tithes, speak in tongues, constantly love and forgive, still continue to be stuck with a set of circumstances that they despise or suffer in. I could not understand why people who are rude, hateful, and angry seem to have money to travel, beautiful families, and can buy whatever they want, and experience life more abundantly than we church folks. Why are there countries that continue to kill one another over religion, sexual orientation, tribe, and status? These were my questions (and so many more) to God. God/Universe/Holy Spirit answered by showing me how I co-created the life I now live by walking into the life I prayed for since I was a child.

Today I am grateful I decided to live. The suicide letter to my daughters was only because I wanted the pain to stop and felt like I had no other way out. I am here today because a little voice inside of me asked, "If you die, who will take care of your children?" I answered, "No one." That was all it took. I have always believed that the answers to all our questions are in the eyes of our children. I chose to live for my daughters and do the best I could to finish college. I made a decision that changed my entire life, and today I live a life that I prayed for and took leaps of faith to get here. I took whatever job I could, I worked my way through the ranks, sold my clothes and shoes, and took abuse to get here. Now I have learned the key to all of it: the energy of love that is inside me and all of us!

Dedication

This book is dedicated to my children. You two have accompanied me on this journey, whether you liked it, loved it, or hated it. My babies! You are my inspiration and motivation to become all that I am. You have inspired me with an undying desire to create more portals to give and receive love in this world. I acknowledge I did not always make the healthiest choices in my life or yours. Just know I was doing the best I could with the knowledge I had at that time. However, it turns out all the pain and all the moves were for a greater purpose. I love you always.

To my mother, thank you for raising me to be the resilient woman I am today. You always taught me to focus on my education and to become independent, so I would not have to hold my hand out to men for money. You also taught me to take those negative words that were thrown my way as motivation, and I gained the power of forgiveness and compassion for others. You always said, "Do the right thing, and the right thing will follow." I love you, Mom, for giving me life and always having the ear to listen to me whenever I thought I was in trouble. I will always be grateful for you. I love you!

To my aunt who took me under her wings when I was a little girl and gave me so much love and attention. Over the years, I watched you and your husband show what love should feel and look like. As a little girl, I watched how you were so affectionate to me, and today you are still that beacon of light in my world. I truly thank you for giving me unconditional love, even after I overfed and killed your boyfriend's fish when I was a kid. You have always loved me, and I will forever be grateful for you.

To my grandmother, thank you for teaching me the power of prayer and the power of words. "There is life and death in the tongue" is what you taught me as a young child. You planted a seed in me the day you kneeled down in front of me, held my hands together in front of my little body, and taught me to say, "Thank you, Jesus," repeatedly. Today I have learned those words alone have been the most powerful three words anyone could have ever taught me. I thank you for loving me and instilling the attitude of gratitude in me. I thank God for blessing me with a grandmother who is filled with so much faith and love for all. I love you so much, and I will always be grateful for you and the gifts you blessed me with—the gift of faith and believing all things are possible, and, of course, the power of love!

To my father, I know your body left us on January 26, 2015, but I feel your presence. I understand now, Daddy. I know now you did not ask for what was given to you as a young boy growing up in Tennessee. I understand now when you started your family, you were doing the best you could. I thank you for always providing and loving us the best way you knew how. I know you are a part of everything. I love you always, Daddy! You taught me to be tough and to stand up for myself. You loved me, and I see this now, and I forgive you.

I understand that the pain we experience can make us or break us, but it is our choice what it will do *for us*. We all have the power to take our own pain and expand our imagination to co-create the life we desire, because this is our birthright! We must recognize the emotions of a groaning spirit and have the courage to move forward toward our own destiny. In other words, walk in faith.

~ Buffy

A Letter to My Daughters

October 16, 2011

To my children,

I love you with all my heart. I can only pray my spirit will always be with you. I am sorry that I had to end my life, but I am no good for either of you. My life has not been the greatest, and the mistakes I made proved to be too hard for me to live in this world. I am tired of fighting to give you both a life with me in peace. I can't take care of both of you on my own. I haven't been able to find a job to get us out of this house. I wish I could give you two the world, but I haven't been able to come through for you. I don't know why life is so hard for me, but I feel like a nobody. This is why I want you both to finish school and learn math and science. I never had an opportunity to learn these subjects from the day I entered kindergarten. And I am so far behind that I can't catch up. It's the reason I wasn't successful in nursing school, and I can't get in now.

I feel so hopeless. Being here with your father over the years has killed a part of me that I will not be able to get back. I don't know who or what I am because I completely submerged my trust in him. I did things in our relationship I am not proud of. But I just wanted to be loved, wanted, desired, respected, and accepted by someone. I realize that no one could ever do this but God. And now I just want to go home to be with Him. This world is filled with so much hate and hurt—it is more than I can bear.

This battle I'm fighting is worthless, as I now know my walk is already written ...

Life was a bitch, and I was ready to check out. I will admit, I hit rock bottom and reached my breaking point. At the time of writing this letter, I had no idea how I was going continue to live with my current life circumstances, because I had been born and lived my entire life in fear.

Preawakening

My eyes have witnessed so much shit. I had no idea my childhood surroundings were conditioning my subconscious mind and would someday play out like a movie of my life. Somehow, I fought for the courage and faith to rise above molestation, depression, poverty, panic attacks, low self-esteem, speech and grammar problems, abandonment, illiteracy, narcissistic abuse, codependency, physical abuse, financial abuse, and psychological abuse and betrayal.

Then I became a genius, in my opinion—a college graduate, an amazing mother, and an oncology senior clinical research associate who travels the world. I monitor cancer trials for chemotherapy to get FDA approved, and now I'm an author. I live on an island in Florida as a single mom, I have tickets to every NFL and NBA game, as well as concerts and events just about anywhere.

But here's the thing—I have observed people with amazing love suffer and struggle with drug addiction, suicide, homicide, prostitution, domestic abuse, molestation, abandonment, schizophrenia, drug dealing, gangs, imprisonment, home raids, poverty, powerlessness, strokes, diabetes, hypertension, psychological abuse, physical abuse, and many others.

I now realize this is no longer a coincidence to me. So my question is—how can people who were created in the image and likeness of God create a mess in their lives and around the world? Do we really understand and accept our birthright as God's birthright too? I think we have, but the issue is that many of us were born into circumstances that co-created a

1

life of hell by default. They have no idea who they truly are and that their inner thoughts and core beliefs are creating their outer world—period!

When I woke up from my hell, I was aware of another dimension in my mind, but I moved to another state before it all happened. Some scientists will call this a quantum leap. I also noticed my experience on this Earth was my own experience. The people around me experienced this Earth according to their own perception.

I have learned that my energy attracts my experiences. I understand now why my family and friends have no idea of the illusion and programming they are under or how to get out. Then again, how can you want to bow out of a delusion if you have no idea you are in one? It is easier to look around and feel the signs of hardship and poverty than to imagine a new world for yourself. You are so caught up in your own wrong perception of how things will always be! No wonder you feel stuck.

I finally figured out why Jesus and other enlightened teachers were teaching us to "walk by faith and not by sight." I found that moving helps because of the intentions and energy behind the actions. To be honest, that is how I unconsciously manifested new journeys in my life. I moved to another state, quit a job (or unconsciously got myself fired) with the intentions of starting a new life each time.

The day I woke from my false perception about myself and my life, I experienced a physical change to my body. I was home, lying in bed, and out of nowhere, the joints in my body locked up. I became temporarily paralyzed and was taken to the ER by my then boyfriend. In the ER, the staff ran a series of tests but found nothing wrong. Once I made it back home, I did my own research and was able to locate a woman who posted a YouTube video about her awakening and the physical change to her body. The doctors could not find anything medically wrong with her—just like what happened to me.

As I continued to look for answers to this event called "awakening," I discovered that all the studying and research I was doing was changing my subconscious mind. The more knowledge I acquired, the more enlightened I became. Then I felt the cells in my body rushing around, physically changing. After that, there was a blanket of calmness, and I accepted this experience as my own awakening.

I was very serious about knowing more about my power, so I could help myself in order to help my mother, my children, and my family. I began reading any book that covered the power of the mind, every day for six years. While I read, I applied what I was learning. I worked on my mind day and night. As I did that, my skin changed, my body changed, my energy changed, my money changed, the people in my life changed, and my home life changed. I no longer experienced my yearly flu or cold, I gained more peace with the absence of certain people, and I had the courage to leave an abusive relationship and to speak my mind. Most importantly, I had the courage to live the way I wanted to—in love and in peace, even if that meant being alone with the Lord, which really is amazing and glorious.

Who Am I? God/Universe/ Holy Spirit Answers!

I n 2011, I was in the darkest place of my life. My mind was fixated on how to survive. At the time, I had no idea that my own perceptions about life were creating my experiences, and one bad thing after another continued to occur. I never knew I had the power to rescue myself. Yet here I am today.

A few days after writing that suicide letter, I decided to follow the words my grandmother taught me when I was a child: Be grateful and say, "Thank you, Jesus." And so I did, but one day my patience ran out. I picked up my Bible to find answers, but I could not find them in this holy book. I became very frustrated; and there I was, alone in my bedroom, when I broke down. I was done with it all, and so I cried out loud to God and slammed my Bible shut. "Something is not right with this," I said. I continued my cry for help, and as my tears flowed, so did questions to God. "Lord, who am I? Why am I here? Why did you create me to only suffer? Lord, please show me who I am! Lord, please show me the truth!" I was tired of feeling like a puppet on a string with God.

I soon found out that God was listening to me. He had always been listening. I found out later I was simply loved unconditionally, and I was far from being a puppet on a string. I was greater than I knew and bigger than I could possibly imagine.

Miracles from God/ Universe/Holy Spirit

In 2012, only one year after writing that suicide letter to my children, I walked into a life that was something greater than I could have ever imagined. As I read over my journals, I realized all the things I wrote and thought about were handed to me after I decided to take a chance and relocate in order to make money to provide for my kids. I literally walked into the sum total of all my prayers. I had been experiencing synchronicity and manifestation, and for a long time, I didn't know it—not until I reflected on my journals and saw a pattern.

From there, I researched what had happened to me *and realized I was manifesting events*. When I became conscious of this, I was finally able to see who I was, according to God and not according to what the world was showing me. God allowed me to see that my life was a mix of all my thoughts, going all the way back to when I was a child, then an adolescent, then a teenager, and now as an adult. I began to understand the quote I learned as a child, "Thou art with me," was true. God pulled the blinders away from my eyes so I could truly see for myself that I was actually co-creating my life with Him. In other words, because I am everything in the eyes of God, I was becoming who I believed and experiencing what I believed and attracting who I was.

The Lord allowed me to experience what scientists call a quantum leap, but in church we called it a *leap of faith*, or stepping out with faith and speaking life into yourself. I was receiving blessings, miracles, and manifestations of experiences, people, and events, without trying to obtain anything; just striving to live a life of peace, provide for my kids on my own, and get my children in a healthier environment. I was doing the best I could, and God felt that.

As I dug a little deeper into my life journey, I recalled that when I was thirteen, I received my first manifestation. However, I was in a survival-consciousness mode and could not see how everything fit when it came to God. Even so, you can only see what you are aware of, and I had no idea or ever heard of the words *universe, manifestation,* and *synchronicity* until I was thirty-six years old, and that awareness happened after I moved to Florida with my daughters. Regardless of my ignorance at the time, my lack of knowing did not hinder me. I learned that my present and habitual situation was made by me, and I was finally able to see how I co-created hell in the first place. I learned that the number-one issue was me!

When I made it out of Hell, I cried like an infant being held in the arms of her mommy. It was at that moment when I knew for the first time in my life that I was loved, and I had a chance to co-create a better life for my children and me.

I finally knew God was my parent, provider, protector, and friend, 24/7. He's been doing this since the day I was born. I learned that I am everything and everyone. Even when I was acting like a fool and making decisions out of fear, I was still loved and blessed, and when I experienced co-creating with hell through my own manifestations, I was blind to the energy I was putting out there. I found out later that I had so many other gifts than the miracles I was expecting. I found out I had the same power that Jesus said I had. Thank you, Jesus!

Church from the Hood

Like so many, I suffered from a mental delusion that seemed real, and I discovered I was living in hell right here on Earth. This went completely against everything I had been taught. I was taught hell was a place I would go if I did not get right with God. God showed me hell was what I was creating when I had or reacted out of my own fear-based thoughts. In other words, I learned not to do anything to anyone I didn't want to experience myself. Energy cannot be destroyed; that shit just comes back to you, and you never know the time or place.

The church I attended in Indiana was truly lost and probably still is, unfortunately. I remember singing in the choir, songs like, "If I Suffer, I'll Get Eternal Life," and I would watch the congregation cry with their hands up in the air, saying in unison, "Thank you, Lord, I am not worthy!"

Wait! What? Was that an affirmation for failure? Then all the men and women would run around the church screaming, with everyone shouting and speaking in tongues as the church music played, and the Holy Ghost would take over them. But there was an issue with this scene for me. According to my pastor, in order for me to go to heaven when I die, I have to be free from all my sins, have the Holy Ghost in my heart, and speak in tongues to have the favor of God in my life. But I had some conflicts in my own spirit. Last Sunday, didn't you say, Pastor, that God said, "Come as you are"?

So, here I am at the church, not feeling worthy enough for God's good grace. All these rules and commandments that I could not follow; and so, I felt like I was not loved by God, who created me, and now I was unworthy. I was nowhere close to having the Holy Ghost, and I certainly did not speak in tongues. No matter how much I prayed for the Holy Ghost or asked for it, I never received it in the way I have seen others receive it.

I remember not feeling worthy at the altar call, while I watched the pastor pray over people by touching their heads to rebuke an evil spirit from them. I stood there in awe, as I watched everyone faint from the pastor's touch—except for me. Lord, what is wrong with me?

I thought to myself, *When in Rome, do as the Romans do!* So, one day when the pastor touched my head, I entertained him and fell to the ground, closed my eyes to avoid looking at people, and lay there until the church music stopped. Truth be told, I felt like an idiot when I did it.

But then there was another Sunday that I summoned up the courage to just be myself and not pretend to faint just to please my pastor. What I didn't know was that he had something else in mind. While standing there in front of him, I decided to lock my knees and stand strong. All of a sudden, I was in battle with my pastor, who wanted me to faint to the ground. The taller I stood strong, the more he pushed my head down to get me to topple. It seemed the more I kept resisting his efforts, the harder he would push down on my head. So, I gave up and just fell to the floor and waited until the experience was all over. Really, though, what other choice did I have? He was hurting my neck, for crying out loud, and just like the people pleaser I was, I was more concerned with not making him look foolish. If I knew then what I know now, I would have said, "Pastor, I have no need or desire to faint on the floor, and I honestly don't believe your hands are more powerful than my own. By the way, you owe me an apology for pushing me down when you felt my resistance." Love and light equal truth. Smile.

I went as far as taking a class to speak in tongues. Can you imagine standing in a room among other professional tongue speakers and teachers who are all there to teach me and others how to speak in tongues? During the class, I was told to say whatever came to my mind. So, I did … I blurted out whatever came to mind, but I knew in my heart it made absolutely no sense. As I continued fake speaking in tongue, I decided to take a sneak peek at my instructors and thought to myself, *You so fake, Buffy.*

Before the tongue-speaking class ended, I already decided I would never go back. So yes, I never felt good enough for the glory of God at that time. Today, I understand my childhood church and the churches I visited were all doing the best they could with their own perceptions of God and how to be blessed by Him. I got lucky that it wasn't too late. God made me realize that everything I had done on my own personal journey brought me to finding Him.

Perception

My perception of life was the sum total of what I had seen, heard, inherited through DNA, passed through the energy of my mother, and picked up through generations. My perception also comes from my church, my community, television, media, and practically every private and personal gathering I have ever participated in. Some may call this perception a generational curse, and I believe it is, but I found so many others who mirrored the same situations from mothers who did not raise their children.

From my own experiences and from other women and men I have worked with, I now believe that these so-called curses are passed through the wombs of mothers, and the pain and emotions were thrust upon us for the nine months we were preparing to be born. I learned this to be true after one of my children started manifesting the things I hated as a child and the pain I carried inside. I watched my first love manifest my fear and experience all my fears. Who knew that what I allowed myself to look at, feel, and attach beliefs to was being soaked up in my subconscious mind? Not me. If I knew, I would have protected my mind or made conscious decisions to pick and choose what I believed.

I wish we knew this as children, before becoming parents. We could have saved ourselves a lot of heartache. That is the main reason why I am writing this book. I wish my mother knew before she had any of us.

Side note: You have free will to pick and choose what you want to believe in by focusing on that belief. However, God had something much greater in store for you. Who knew that our subconscious mind (spirit) created the world around us, including the people who we think are our enemies? WTF? Truth is, there is no enemy except the enemy within you, and that fear shows up (in your perception) through people you know and even those you love. Your own perception of who you are is based on your own fear, brokenness, and what you love. People will only give you what you fear, what you love, what you feel, what you believe about yourself, what you think about them, and how you see others. Therefore, you must love your enemy. These people are the reflections of your fears and limited beliefs. Your enemy will go away once you allow that fear to come to the surface and heal it on an energetic level. Jesus taught us to guard our hearts, for what flows from it are the issues of the world. But no child has any control over the circumstances of what type of life they are born into.

My subconscious mind created a world full of children, men, and women who would abandon me, abuse me, betray me, lie to me, and make me feel I was never enough, unimportant, and irrelevant. I felt like this from the time I entered elementary school, and this feeling stayed with me for many, many years. In other words, I kept experiencing the same feeling from my childhood trauma and how I always felt as a child, completely invisible and unimportant.

I attracted people who reflected how I secretly felt about myself and the deep-seated hurt I carried, growing up. The family I was raised in had many issues, and love was not there, so I went seeking it from anyone who would like me, starting in kindergarten when I took twenty dollars from my mother to pay some girl to be my friend. Yes, I did that; when I entered kindergarten, I was already broken. Not realizing my experiences were emotionally recreated, just like at home, I felt unimportant, unseen, unwanted, abandoned, and alone. That's exactly what I attracted in elementary and middle school.

At the same time, at home I felt I had to give up something to be loved by my family. So, I drew pictures for my mother, I sang to her, and I followed her to the bathroom. I needed her, but I understand now how much she needed me. She gave what she could. Later on, I learned that looking for love from others only lowered my self-esteem and self-worth. I thought I was looking to get love from others, but instead I attracted those who did not love themselves and could not love me in return. Like attracts like, right? Something else I learned was that I was the gifted one, and all the love I had in me was because I am an empath.

Growing up, I didn't feel smart at all. I learned nothing in school and later struggled to learn all I needed to know in college. I spent fourteen years in a mentally abusive, financially abusive relationship and was paid to have sex with my ex when I refused to do so after being mentally abused. I left that relationship and attracted a man who was all I ever wanted until the day he did something I hated. He chose his best friend over me and told me he needed her, and that she was his rib. I had already moved in with him with my two daughters and was trying to raise his daughter as my own.

The abuse was frequent and painful. Once he threw a large bottle full of coffee creamer at me when I asked if he would help with the laundry. His abuse extended to things like choking me until I almost passed out, throwing a shower caddy at me while I was naked in the shower, and allowing anyone to speak poorly about me to him, all the while checking out and entertaining anything with a vagina. He wanted me in the strip club with him and asked me about doing threesomes. When he started hanging out with my childhood friend without me, I knew I had reached a breaking point. After seven years of continued disrespect and abuse, I finally removed myself from a situation that I did not deserve to be in.

What finally did it for me? It was a powerful prayer. I spent the entire day at home crying, talking to my mother about how trauma is passed on to our children. On that day, I cried out to her, I forgave her and understood her and my dad, and I knew it was authentic because I felt so much compassion. Afterward, I laid down in my prayer closet, with the door shut and in the dark; I allowed my heart to break and moan and groan about everything that broke it. I gave forgiveness to myself and others and released all ill feelings. Later, in the middle of the night, I received several calls. My boyfriend of seven years was found unconscious at a casino. Once I arrived at the hospital, I watched him as he lay there. I was flooded with doubt and questions. *What is really going on?* I knew we had been arguing, but this was too much.

Later that day, his belongings were released to me. I kept his phone and sent his other personal belongings home. His password was easy to figure out, but then again, my intuition was strong. I decided to dig deeper into his phone. What I learned was hurtful. I found out that my boyfriend (and the love of my life) had a whole life that I was not aware of. It turned out that all this time, he was baiting me. He would always say he was not ready for marriage because we could not find a stable footing. Then I realized that he purposely started fights with me to get out of the house. I found this so-called enlightened man was involved in orgies with his friends, frequented strip clubs (and lied about it), and was now a cocaine addict, and at the moment he was in the hospital after having a stroke. I also realized that I attracted circumstances that mirrored what I felt about myself and it felt like the same pain I had with my dad and my ex. It was the feeling of not being enough, not being lovable. I was learning that my needs mattered and I was important.

I also learned later on that hair and makeup could not cover my broken spirit. These men in my life were narcissists, and I was an empath.

As I grew more spiritually, I realized the origin of my foundation. I also realized that I was living a lie and confirmed what I always knew as a little girl: this life I was born into was not what it was supposed to be. We did not come to Earth to suffer at all. My ancestors who were slaves never knew this, except my grandmother, who found Jesus after moving from Mississippi to Indiana. My grandmother knew the one thing that drives each of us every day, and that is the power of words. She warned me to never allow anyone to speak over me, including doctors. I have come to understand that for generations, all of my family were broken off spiritually from the highest energy of the entire universe. That was *love* and their birthrights.

I am not talking about the kind of love you share among your spouse, children, family, and extended family. I am talking about the kind of love that creates the kingdom of God around us. I am talking about self-love and the power you hold but were taught that it is outside of you and only Jesus had it. But Jesus told you who you were. The greatest mastermind ever was destroying the perception of so many people, causing them to hate themselves and become bitter and broken to the point of losing their inner light, a light they never knew was their power—their love for themselves and their love for others. That is the most powerful light in our lives.

What saved me was understanding God's love for me and loving the Lord, keeping my faith in Him, and knowing His power in my life. He taught me that something *was* wrong with the circumstances I was born into.

The Lord met me at my lowest point to show me the pain I endured and created my prayer: no weapon formed can prosper because I am more powerful than I know.

Recently, a client of mine asked me how I made it out okay after all of the abuse and destruction I experienced. I told her, "No matter what I have been through and what others have done to me, I never stopped loving all people, including people I did not know, and I never gave up on myself. On my journey, the biggest thing I had to learn was to love myself unconditionally. Everything after that became easier."

My Work

My work was filtering through my own spiritual illusions and beliefs, breaking agreements made unconsciously and understanding the truth about physical reality and false beliefs. I found out the hard way that it was my own predominant thoughts and subconscious mind creating the world around me; my own beliefs manifesting into physical reality. How did I find out my thoughts were creating my world? I knew because I was living my thoughts and manifested things and people that I only thought of in my head and without praying for it. When I consciously chose to have better thoughts, my days became better, almost like heaven here on Earth. I also noticed each day would happen according to what I was thinking and feeling.

For example: I was deep in thought while thinking of Anthony Hamilton, one of my favorite R&B artists. On the same day, thirty minutes later, I was redirected to another gate while at the airport and walked straight into Anthony Hamilton after listening to his song, "Amen." I was able to tell him how much I loved his new song.

There were other surprise instances. One day I was home watching *The Braxton Family* and all this talk about Birdman and Toni Braxton being together. The very next day he was in my way while I was looking for jewelry.

I was on the plane thinking about Oprah, and as soon as I made it off the plane and turned right, Stedman, her life partner, was walking my way. I was at a restaurant in Florida and one in Vegas, and Trey Songz seemed to follow me after listening to his music. Wyclef popped up after watching him and his wife on TV, and NeNe Leakes was boarding my plane the next day after watching her on the *Real Housewives of Atlanta*.

God showed me I could co-create anything. I love tacos, and there was not one taco restaurant when I first moved to my area. I visualized having lots of taco restaurants to choose from. Now there are currently taco restaurants all around me, and two are walking distance from me.

Stuff like this was happening all the time. There were also a couple of times I did not want an interview for a position and just wanted the job with sponsors within my company; the meetings were canceled, and I got the job. Now, the biggest manifestation will remain a secret, for now.

Fear (Sin)

Most of us walk around in our own little worlds, clueless as to why our lives got to be the way they are. Whether you realize it or not, our core beliefs about ourselves, each other, and the world are our own individual creations and created with the force we call God. I discovered that God does not choose for us; rather, we live out our own beliefs. Yup! We are what we believe—literally, and we will experience what we think about ourselves, others, and the world!

I know many have heard others say, "Well, I'll believe it when I see it!" Well, those folks will never see anything, and you can consider them the walking dead. You must believe in the present moment—who you want to be, as if you are that person already and it is already done. Whatever you want to experience happens in your mind first like a movie. As you move with action and feeling, you will become and experience that which you hold inside of yourself.

Healing

It is important to understand your own foundation to heal yourself from false beliefs in order to recreate your own life. Only you know what is good for you, who your true self is, and what kind of life is in alignment with who God created us all to be. That is to live an abundant life and to see people and the world through love. I had to *intend* on seeing love in people and all things in order to see my world with love. I also had to walk away from old energies that drained me and did not align with my true self.

Currently, I still work in oncology research, and I actually started a clinical trial on myself. As I read different books and applied them to my life, I began to change and consciously control my energy through gratitude and focusing on what and who I love. I began to see my world change around me. That is when I concluded that there was something to this. I found the thoughts we think day to day truly co-create our daily experiences. The way I felt day to day would bring in people feeling the same way in my life that day. So, I worked daily to have better thoughts. I made new agreements by feeding my spirit/brain new information through reading and focusing on what I wanted to experience. My world changed, but not everyone in my family and my friends was changing with me. So, some energies shifted away and some became closer. In this process, I learned there is no such thing as one size fits all in life. That is, all of our lives vary because all of our perceptions, beliefs, dreams, and fears are different.

Some of you may be on the path of consciousness/awakening right now. Some of you may be living in a dream state of fear/hell, just like I was until 2013. I was completely blind and was taught unconsciously by my loved ones to think in a mind-set of fear. I was focused on the current lack in my life and all the things I did not have. Most times, I heard and believed in the perception of "what next bad thing was going to happen," and I was completely unaware that I was thinking in the mind-set of fear and bringing all that negative stuff into my life.

Thinking in fear is very tricky! A fear-based mind-set is programmed to think that way (but not on purpose) by our families, friends, and communities. In my family, the fear was due to slavery; we were born into fear, which is the primary reason for sin—you know, those things we do that hurt ourselves and others, and then we ask for forgiveness later? What you do not know are the reasons why. I can tell you why I sinned. I sinned because I had no idea I had the power to literally move things with my mind, the power to think about what I wanted and it appeared; and when I prayed, God heard me the first time because, just like you, I am everything and everyone.

We all have experienced some of our power. So, my question to you is, have you ever thought of someone and they either called you or you ran into them? I know the answer, but this is an example of how we unintentionally use our power. If I knew about this power, I would have never acted out in fear, but rather in faith of knowing I could do and have all things. And if I knew what I gave came right back to me, I would have lived more authentically because my true nature is love, and that is truly what I wanted to give but did not know how.

So many of us have been taught not to ask the universe/God questions. I was taught not to question God, but I did ask why my family had to live like we were living. I am grateful I asked the question. I would not be here today if I did not ask God my questions. I was ready to leave this Earth and I think it is crazy for us to suffer because we are afraid to ask why. I would have never known that heaven could exist right now and where I stand if I did not ask all those questions to where I am at this moment.

I now believe that along the way we are being taught to ask questions because we know the universe will answer them. I know for sure because it brought me to 2003 after getting food poisoning and passing out. In doing so, I experienced something phenomenal. I remember falling into a dark space, but my spirit was praying and asking God to spare my life. My other words to Him were, *not now and not like this* as I saw visions of my parents and my children. The more I prayed, the more I was lifted into consciousness again.

When I finally opened my eyes, a voice inside of me said, "Go outside." A friend was with me, and I informed her I needed to go outside. When I walked outdoors, I saw the air was some sort of barely visible frequency, as if the clear ocean was surrounding me. I saw in this frequency the cars, the streetlights, the trees, and the ground moving. Then the voice in me said, "I am everything, I am the trees, I am the ground you walk on." I was afraid and confused at that time and started screaming and crying. I had no idea what I experienced until 2013, after my awakening.

Unfortunately, there are millions around the world who do not understand this hidden knowledge and all their birthrights, no matter where they are in the world, their current health status, or their present financial situation. We all have free will to choose who we want to be and what we want to experience in our lives every day. I learned we must have faith and confidence in ourselves and that we are already worthy because we were born. The question is, "How do I change a reality that I am currently in?"

Limited Beliefs

There is no reason to think with limited beliefs once you understand who you truly are. I lived with the results of changing my beliefs, and for almost seven years now, I have been doing the work toward renewing my mind and documenting how my life has changed! I come with my testimony to let you know I used to live in a mind-set that gave me hell right here on Earth. I am here to testify with the assistance of God, through the power of prayer, and finally believing in myself, that I have been living a life through a constant shift and have witnessed a world that looks like and feels like my own personal heaven in my own personal life each day. Unfortunately, the boyfriend I manifested did not grow with me. Truth is, by the time we separated, I was not the same energy I was when we first met. Everyone grows at their own pace.

Moving Forward

My life started to change when I began asking questions. I was able to come to this place of understanding and true knowing of who I am. Hopefully, as you read my story, you will begin to learn how to remove your own filters and understand the long-term effects of your own culture and upbringing from generations and generations of behaviors, beliefs, and actions over which you had no control.

You can come to your own understanding of why you made it out of the projects or the hood or maybe overcame challenging obstacles or a fatal disease. Perhaps you will also understand why some think that gangbanging, killing, raping, prostituting, and robbing people are acceptable ways to get what you want.

Many have come and gone and never realized that there was a spiritual battle within them that caused one to live on the *dark side of life*. What do I mean by the dark side of life? Well, most of us were born into a lifestyle filled with a constant state of fear, brought on by negative thoughts. It feels real to you, and those thoughts become your reality. You can dream a nightmare or dream of love, but in both cases, you have to retrain your subconscious mind. This was a struggle for me to get out of because I kept getting caught in experiencing life through my interpretation of what I observed each day, and I reminded myself of my own lack of resources, limitations to opportunities to do anything, a weak bank account, multiple illnesses of people around me, and feeling helpless because I felt alone. I felt unloved, not good enough, incompetent, and the list goes on and on. All of this. Until I realized it was all a bad dream!

I work with people now, and I have to admit, some will never overcome their own frustration, angst, and pity until they understand that they are literally in two worlds. There is the spiritual world (your mind) and the physical world (Earth)—which is the manifestation of your mind. The key is to understand that whatever your mind believes in the spiritual world will be manifested in the physical form on Earth. You were already informed that you have dominance over the Earth through the Word of God.

Once you understand your gift, you will realize you do not have to cheat, lie, steal, kill, gangbang, rob, hate, prostitute, buy sex, fight, take drugs, or commit suicide. You will no longer think that you are not smart enough, good enough, or that you need to change yourself for others or worry about other people's opinions, or even worry about money. We all are truly one! Just different extensions of each other, but we communicate telepathically without knowing it. We all are one with the Spirit! Because you are literally the air, baby!

I have been quietly living this way. More importantly, this is what my life has been ever since I decided to live in love. Now, I am not the only one out here. I had no idea who I was or what God put in me, or what I have been doing all my life. After stepping out in faith and then walking back into all my thoughts and dreams, I realized I was blessed with miracles.

Born to Heal

When I was a young child, I lived inside my mind to escape the hardships and abuse going on in my home with my family. It was constant. But I used my imagination to escape from all the bad things going on. In my late thirties, I understood what Jesus meant when he said, "Become like children." I must say, I managed to unconsciously manifest all the things I wanted to experience, and I became stronger in my power as I studied more subjects about others who also experienced miracles. The only problem was that I did not find information that could assist me in knowing more about the foundation I was born into.

As a little girl, I used to look at myself in the mirror all the time, and a little voice would say, "Something is not right about this life my family is living." Still staring into the mirror, I would ask myself, "Who am I?" and "Why doesn't my family have the kind of life I see on TV?" Turns out that little voice has been guiding me all my life, and now I understand it was the Holy Spirit in me, as me.

After making a faith-based decision, I moved to Florida on October 19, 2012, and this decision would later lead me to understand who I was and my awakening. I learned how I manifested the visions of my life that I wrote about, daydreamed about, and imagined since I was a teenager. I realized how much I was loved. The epiphany was so powerful that I developed a hunger to know more, especially if there were others out there like me. I became very thirsty for knowledge and would buy every book on

31

the topic of the power of the mind, to better understand who I was. Turns out, this was my purpose and destiny, as God has been providing me with visions, whispers, and dreams for years.

So, after all these years, I decided to come out of my closet and write the book that began when the idea of a book was placed in my spirit during a dream as a teenager. In my dream, I was to save some girl who was screaming for help. Turns out God knew my life journey would assist others through my testimony on how my thoughts became my reality. My pain was my purpose! This is what I learned, and it is for you: no matter what others say or do, you will come out on top. It happens when you decide to love yourself, love everyone, give what you desire, have a vision, and believe all things are possible!

Our Fathers on 2600 Jackson Street

My family are decedents of slavery. My DNA comes from Nigeria, Europe, Ireland, Asia, Scandinavia, and 6 percent of me is unknown. My perception about life was created through fear by my ancestors, who lived and later worked in cotton fields as sharecroppers in Tennessee, Mississippi, and God only knows where else.

My father was a handsome man, funny, witty, and charming. He loved to cook and watch his cowboy shows. He worked hard and seemed to be well liked by all who came to visit our home, and was the greatest to all who we would visit in his hometown in Tennessee. However, I experienced firsthand the true spirit of my father.

My father worked hard to pay bills and put food on the table, but he was an alcoholic, had mistresses, bought himself nice things to wear, and was physically abusive. Often, he would leave on a Friday, which was payday, and return a day or so later after being with his woman. He talked to other women on the phone while my mom was at work. Once, I approached him at his girlfriend's apartment, and he pulled guns out on us and threatened to kill all of us if we kept getting up in his business.

He only gave me attention when company came from out of town. He was a good actor. But I also experienced a dad who would tell me that I was going to college. He followed me as protection when men started looking and stopping me on my way to school. He killed to save a family member of mine. There were times when he told us we were wrong and would sit around and talk and joke with us. I love my daddy! He built an alpha female and made me very strong and forced me to stand up for myself. But he added unhealthy beliefs to my subconscious mind without knowing it.

I did not understand my father until after he died. His aunt later revealed to me that my dad's father was the same way, except he never provided for his family, was a womanizer, had children outside of his marriage, was never there for his children, abused his wife and beat her so badly she had to be hospitalized, beat his children, was an alcoholic, and spent time in prison for murdering a man.

And the lineage goes on. My grandfather's sons were like him, and all were alcoholics, womanizers, had children outside of marriage, and were physically abusive to their wives and children—but they thought it was normal. However, they broke one curse (mental perception) that their father lived with, and that was they all managed to work and provide for their families. I asked my aunt why my grandfather was like that. She explained to me that his grandfather on his mother's side of the family, including relatives, were all violent alcoholics. They were the byproduct of their environment (learned behavior from slave master).

Daddy is Home

Most of the fights would break out when my dad did not come home, when asked for money, or when he got caught cheating. I remember how he had to get picked up from his favorite hangout and brought home after a drunken night. Sometimes he would drive himself home and pass out in the driveway, still behind the wheel, until morning. However, when he was home drunk from gin, the fights broke out. I remember how he would curse my mom out, pull her hair, and one time he sat on top of her, beating the hell out of her. Today, no one will dare speak out about this stuff. Even as kids, my mom would remind us, "He is still your father, and you will respect him, or I will beat your ass!"

There were times I would say something and was told to keep my mouth shut to keep the peace, and so I did. Little did my family know that later I would have to recover and heal due to codependency. I would hide in the basement, without saying a word, with pure dread during their fights. As I sat on the basement stairs listening, I felt helpless. Even though I was only five years old, I tried to call the police for help, but I didn't know my address and I didn't know what I was doing, so I couldn't get the help my mom needed. No one ever came.

Through the years, I watched my family members experience all of the abuse, but I could never do anything about it. Every attempt she made to leave him failed; she always came back. I remember thinking to myself that I would never go through such abuse by any man, but I later I relived some of her nightmares. I learned later in life that this was one of my biggest obstacles that I needed to overcome. Because I always tried to keep the peace in our house and feared disappointing her, I had terrible boundaries for myself and allowed people to repeatedly hurt me. Because I am an empath, I was constantly forgiving, and I was not able to let go of the same people who continually violated me, because this was a learned behavior.

Buffy's Darkness

From the day I was born until I left Indiana at the age of eighteen, all was good with my mother's side of the family. However, my home was filled with negative people, negative self-talk, plantation beatings with extension cords, kicks to the body, beatings with shoes, hangers, and tree branches. Guns with laser sights were pointed at heads by someone who was supposed to love us and protect us, hair was pulled, and heads were beaten against walls. But what happens in the house stays in the house.

At school I was bullied. I was called names like *honky* at home because of my light skin and *pee girl* at school because my clothes had the stench of urine from the pallet I shared that was on the floor. I was told I was not liked because I acted like a boy, and I was forced to fight others against my will. If I refused, I would later get beaten up.

I witnessed countless episodes of domestic abuse against someone I love and by someone who said *I love you* all the time, a father who would bring home ice cream and food from restaurants just for himself. I witnessed theft to have basic needs met, adultery for many years, illegitimate children, and codependency. I experienced children raising children and a role model who never took time for me. My parents did not teach me how to read, write, or ride a bike, help with homework, or have anyone at home to assist me in learning. My dad was too drunk to attend my high school graduation and refused to attend my college graduation. Once again, it gave me the energy of pain, of not feeling good enough, not important enough, or relevant.

Before leaving Indiana, everything I experienced in my childhood gave me my perspective on life, and from there I built my path, one step at a time. Through it, I created a new perception. Everything I experienced, saw, and heard steered my life into poverty, lack of necessities, limitations, homelessness, physical abuse, financial abuse, mental abuse, and panic attacks, due to anxiety and being promiscuous. At the time, I did not know that all of the scenes I was witnessing as a child and all the broken words and negative people around me were building my subconscious life, as well as my beliefs as a woman. As a result, I lived my life and experienced what my family instilled in me unintentionally and unconsciously because, through all those years, these were now beliefs embedded into my subconscious. I also finally realized that it was impossible for my parents to give me what they did not have: self-love.

Buffy's Contrast

My contrasting experiences were things that made me want the opposite experiences in life than what I grew up in. Later, throughout this book, you will find that all my contrasts led to prayers and many manifestations that continue every day throughout my life.

In little Buffy's world, I used to hate sleeping on the floor on a pile of blankets pissed out. I hated being sent to school and made fun of because of the urine stench. I was ignored by the popular and pretty girls for not having the best clothes and shoes, and acting too much like a boy, in their opinion. Truth is, I did act like a boy, and boys were the only friends I had in my neighborhood. Besides, none of the boys at school gave me the time of day.

I did not like the smell of dog poop coming from my daddy's hunting dogs that stayed in the backyard. I did not want to see my father being abusive or lining us up for a "just-in-case-you-did-something-bad ass-whipping."

For years I had a secret resentment toward my father. I did not want to experience the abandonment and felt that I never had the opportunity to voice how it all made me feel. I just wanted to say, "I do not like the way we love each other."

I did not want to experience the abuse from my dad and having my head beaten against the wall or asked to strip down to my panties and bra in order to be whipped with tree branches. I did not like the fact that I could not read or do math.

I attended speech therapy in elementary school because I did not know how to speak properly and use grammar correctly. I hated the fact that I was emotionally broken from being bullied in elementary and throughout middle school. I was told and treated as if I was never worthy or good enough. I was disregarded by some teachers in elementary school who would lie across me and cause me to get paddled and not allow me to join the clubs that all the pretty and popular girls were in. I was never given a reason why I could not be a part their group. I felt like a nobody at home and at school.

Buffy's Vision

I envisioned the love I wanted to feel, along with a beautiful home, joy, freedom, parents like the ones on TV, and traveling the world as a family; and while the beatings continued, I honestly blanked out and began to sing and dance on Broadway in New York City. My inner world is what saved me. I was living in my imagination, and I stayed in my mind.

Throughout elementary school, I started to pay more attention to how people lived. I remember thinking, *Hey, I want to do that. I want to talk like that. I want to sing like that. I want to dress like that. I want to dance like that, and I want to walk like that.* I did not know at the time that this mind-set would serve me for the greater good years later. I was rebuilding myself and consciously choosing from others what I wanted to be and experience in my life, and all I collected in my mind would later become my life.

Buffy the Spiritual Player

The summer of 1992 was the first transitioning moment for me and the beginning of many journeys that would later bring me to the place I am today.

I had just completed the eighth grade, and I was in my bed, trying to fall asleep. I remember the phone ringing really late at night and my father answering it. Unfortunately, it turned out to be one of my bullies from school. This girl was hell on wheels. Each time she saw me, she would shove herself into me or call me names. I am not sure how she got my parents' phone number, but she decided to prank call my house on the wrong night.

At the time, I could not speak to boys on the phone, and my mother was working the night shift. This girl had the balls to pretend to be a boy and asked to speak to me, and per my dad, she said "Let me to speak to Buffy, Daddio." My father later called me upstairs, pulled out an extension cord, and told me why he was whooping me, adding, "I do not want to hear what you have to say. Turn your ass around." My dad beat me very badly that night.

I ran downstairs back into the basement to my bedroom. As I lay there, I looked at the whipping marks on my arms and legs and the blood blisters on my hands, and I began to cry from the sight of my body. I looked badly beaten this time. I also remember becoming very angry at God. I asked Him, "Why have you forsaken me? Why did you allow him to do this to me?"

As I lay there in my bed for who knows how long, my tears stopped, and my anger subsided. That is when I began to talk to God. All of a sudden, my mind started envisioning what I wanted to do to make myself feel better, and I began thinking of ways to spend as much time away from home as possible. As I prayed, I asked God to heal my body.

I also told myself that once my body healed from the beating, I was going to become a varsity cheerleader in my freshman year of high school. Truth be told, I had never played a sport at school or cheered, but that is what I wanted to do. My mind began to fill up with spectacular ideas. I thought about a crush of mine since elementary school, and I told myself that I was going with Jamie to his Sophomore Star Night Dance when I made it to high school.

I am going to win the trophies for Most Attractive Senior and Best Figure in my senior year. I also told myself that I was going to be homecoming queen. I decided that I would date the captain of the football team and the captain of the basketball team, who happened to be my crush, Jamie.

The Phoniest Senior

When I entered high school, I had already made up my mind that if no one was going to love me, then I was simply going to love myself. When I made it to high school, I loved myself so much that it seemed like everyone wanted a piece of me! There were some who loved me and some who wanted to fight me. But by high school, I had a different kind of focus and mission. That was to keep to myself, work to have money to buy my own clothes and a car, and keep busy to avoid being home as much as possible.

Some may have thought my treatment by others would have made me jaded or mean to people, but no matter what was going on at home, I was just me, and that is—I simply love everyone. I also would stand up for other kids who were being bullied or fight if I needed to protect myself or others. I spoke my mind and stuck to my plan.

I prepared and practiced over the summer prior to school starting. I visualized the kind of cheerleader I would become, and once my legs healed, I was ready. During my tryout, I put everything into it because I wanted it so badly, and I made the junior varsity team. After football season of 1993, I earned my letters and became a varsity cheerleader while still in my freshman year in high school. I predicted this on that night I was crying in my bed after my beating. My elementary crush was now the captain of the basketball team, and yes, Jamie took me to his Sophomore Star Night. But he cheated on me for not giving up my virginity to him, so I decided to make the captain of the football team my boyfriend. My so-called leveling up.

I won all the trophies I said I would win, and with no real effort. I won Most Popular, Best Figure, Most Attractive, Most Flirtatious, and the class of 1996 gave me an additional trophy for "The Phoniest Senior." I accepted that trophy proudly! I even managed to think quickly on my feet and gave my senior class a thank-you speech.

The speech went like this: "To everyone who voted for me, I would like to thank you for voting for me as the Phoniest Senior. I tried my best to be as phony as I possibly could, and it worked. It actually worked! Thank you all!"

I walked off that stage with my Chinese-inspired hair and outfit like a queen and was completely unbothered by this award. At this point in my life, my haters motivated me even more, and I took nothing personally. I paid them no mind because I knew who I was and why I was the way I had to be. I did not talk to many people or get caught in drama unless someone bothered someone I loved. I had a mission in life: to save myself and validate me, no matter what.

As I look back on that night I lay in bed with my raw bruises from my father's beating, everything I asked God for came true. I was still clueless as to who I was and my birthright, but I had the greatest high school years a girl could ever want!

Broken Spirit: August 1997

After leaving my parents' home, I spent only one year at college, in Tennessee. I chose this school because my parents did not have the money to send me to a university. The college allowed me to work on campus, which paid for my tuition. When I arrived on campus, the school looked abandoned and probably had one hundred students at the most. I later found out that the school started losing their accreditation right before I started my program, but I had no idea what that meant at the time. I was just grateful to be out of Indiana.

Going off to college was my only goal, with the intentions of making my momma proud. Frankly, I did not really have a bigger vision than that. It was also the first time I was on my own without my family. Unfortunately, it did not last long, because I had issues of feeling not good enough. Truth is, I came to Tennessee with a Bible in my hand and left as a weed smoker and pregnant by a Kappa who would father my firstborn daughter but never meet her. Twenty-one years later, she is still waiting.

I was a mess in college. I had a too-fine boyfriend who was in the marines, and I really loved him. How we met was so weird, but now I understand why our paths crossed, because I can now acknowledge the power of my mind. In 1995, I saw this gentleman on the cover of a newspaper while I was still in high school. He was in his senior year and was the captain of the football team at another high school in Indiana. I circled his picture with a pen. In 1997, right before I left for college, my cousin called, saying her friend's cousin was coming into town and that he was very "cute." I was interested but told her that he would have to come to where I work if he wanted to meet me. At the time, I was working as a shoe salesperson at Sears before I left for college. This man showed up, and when I put my eyes on him, I instantly remembered that he was the guy I circled in the newspaper article in 1995. I told him that. It was love at first sight, until I left for Tennessee.

The Devil is a Liar

While at college, I met a Kappa who had already graduated from KC. He was looking for fresh meat, but I was naive. So, here I was with my unworthy self, impressed by this guy because he was a Kappa. Even though he only showed up to have sex with me, I still felt like I was somebody because I was dating a Kappa. At the time, I was also still speaking to, and being financially supported by, my high school sweetheart, the captain of the football team from high school, who I knew would do anything for me. Unfortunately, he kept trying to control me. It started when we were in high school. He felt like he needed to take on a parental role with me. There were reasons for that, though; he was actually providing for me during that time. He made sure I was always okay at home, bought me things, replaced my torn shoes, and was always there for me. There were times that he would walk in the freezing cold to bring me food. I thought he was the best thing that ever happened to me when we were together, but it all came with a price. I had to be who and what he wanted me to be, and when I did not give him what he wanted, he would punish me by taking back whatever he bought me or decide to break up with me.

I tried to break it off in high school, but after he graduated, he stuck around Indiana, and according to him, he was waiting for me to graduate from high school. One day he saw me walking with another guy after he decided to break it off with me. So, he decided to run in the middle of the street to intentionally get hit by a car. When that didn't work, he ran to someone's yard who had pit bulls, hoping they would attack them. Now, when that did not work, he came over a day or so later to drink the bleach in my family's laundry room. What is really sad is I am the one who received a beating for his actions, so I was definitely over this guy. Or so I thought. He was the guy I tried to get away from but couldn't. In his mind, he owned me because he was the person taking care of me. Truth is, he did take care of me just like a parent, but he did not own me.

Well, this love triangle did not last long. After just eight months away from Indiana, I found out I was pregnant by the Kappa. He had already disappeared before I found out. So here I was, knocked up and living on campus. I called my family, who told me to call the ex-boyfriend because he needed to know so he could go on with his life. I called my grandmother, who told me it was better to marry than for him to burn in hell. I followed my family advice and called my ex-boyfriend, who said he would marry me and raise the child as his own.

I listened to everyone except myself and married him. I thought I had to keep up my good name, and I needed to get married fast before anyone knew that I was having a child and not married. I wanted to avoid the embarrassment to my family. The decision I made to marry someone I was not in love with was out of fear and caused so much heartache. When I told my mother that I did not love him, she said, "You will grow to love him." But I never did, and the way he talked to me and treated my child and me when he got me away from everyone made me pull away from him and look for love everywhere else I could find it.

I entered into a relationship that was psychologically and sexually abusive, including both of us cheating on each other. His verbal abuse and financial abuse pushed me away when I wasn't being codependent and an empath. He was a narcissist, and we were only twenty years old. What the hell did we know? Our relationship was toxic in high school, and our combined homegrown issues from our parents made us very unhealthy for each other. To escape it all, I did what I knew how to do, and that was to repeat the errors of my parents and start smoking cigarettes and look to men to cope. I quietly went through life suffering inside, hanging out with my friends to stay away from home, hiding my issues by looking for people to fulfill the void. What I thought I needed from him was for my ex to talk to me. He actually would curse me out all the time, refuse to touch me, and tell me he did not have time for what I wanted. He would also constantly remind me that my daughter was not his.

Meanwhile, I was still suffering inside, with all the childhood echoes of my dad's voice telling me, "You aren't shit!" and my ex saying, "You aren't shit and will never be shit, and you are just like your dad." In the meantime, I kept attracting men and women who would treat me like I was not shit; instead, they would use me. Let me rephrase that: I would allow men and women in my life to abandon me, hit me, choke me, call me names, fight me for expressing my feelings, have sex with me and never call me again, talk about me behind my back, tell my secrets to others to belittle me, and lie to me. And when I set boundaries, I was not shit!

Lost in the Matrix

I was lost, and I did not love me at all. I mean, why would I love me? Going to church was helping me to be good in order to have the favor of God and His blessings. If I was good enough when I died, I could experience the pearly gates, love and peace called heaven, and when I suffered here on Earth, it would be a sacrifice to God. So, no, I did not love me! I struggled with loving me, and I loved everyone, but I did not know how to love me. All my life, no one taught me how to love me, because no one in my family truly loved themselves.

Today, I understand that what happened in my journey was purposeful, but at the time I could not see it that way. My pain was not my punishment; rather, it was the reflection of all the fear I carried in my subconscious mind and my feelings about me. The journey was God's grace and mercy because the Spirit knew I would be able to heal from all the hell I encountered along the way.

I had to face each of my fears one by one. I now understand all the seeds, such as poverty, childhood abuse, alcoholism, spousal infidelity and abuse, feelings of defeat, not having self-worth, laziness, settling for less, and feeling helpless were spiritual seeds sowed in me from being born in fear. My parents lived in fear and could only give their children the experiences they knew about.

Spiritual Blindness Revealed

All of my fears were deeply rooted in my subconscious mind, creating my reality. I now understand the development of my perception and the creation of my personality were due to the beginning stages of my life. If my dad was healthy and knew about his birthright, he would not have been the man he was, who did the things he did. My dad knew nothing else and did nothing else. My ex learned from his dad, and he knew nothing else and therefore did only what he knew.

I understand now that I unconsciously attracted negative circumstances in my life, attracted toxic relationships that would later leave me more broken than I was before because I kept carrying around the pain of my childhood and past energies of relationships. I see now that *I am energy*, and it all makes sense. My mind was always focused on what I did not have, and this mind-set kept abundance from coming into my life. My need at that time for someone to love me, tell me I was beautiful, that I mattered, and that I am somebody was my only mission, but I did not understand that I could only attract what I felt about me.

My perception led me down a road that continued for sixteen years and attracted more psychological abuse, financial abuse, physical abuse, sexual abuse, and abandonment. I later became very depressed and ended up in the emergency room after experiencing a panic attack, which led to being prescribed antidepressants. I wore my abuse so well that no one knew how much I was suffering at that time in my life. As a child, I learned how to keep things inside. Much like the saying, "What happens in this house stays in this house." I was being abused by my father, and watched my father abusing himself with alcohol, and we did not have permission to talk about it to anyone, not even among ourselves, even now. No one knew what we were going through, and no one knew of our family pain and secrets.

Unfortunately, we learned how to take abuse and pretend like it never happened and continue to forgive him and live life like nothing ever happened. I should have known my purpose back then, because I never kept my mouth shut about the abuse. Later on, I was punished by my father; about six months before he passed away, he said to me, "Me and your mother are considered dead to you, and do not contact us again." My father completely shut me out after calling the police to do a wellness check, after hearing a loved one over the phone having a mental breakdown in their home while one of my daughters was there. Instead of them getting help for them, my family took them to church, and they came back with the same condition.

Days later, after I made the call to the police, my father said that I was stupid and did not know how to be married. I explained to him that my ex was abusive to me. My father let me know that what I was going through "wasn't shit" and that he knew men who would kick my ass, take my money, not work, and also cheat. My response was, "Are those my only options? What about choosing neither and choosing myself and loving myself and being independent?" And that is the choice I made.

The Foundation of My Abusers, Compassion, for They Were Victims
The Apples Do Not Fall Far from the Tree Until You Catch Them

My great-grandfather was murdered by his mother's brother, and his behavioral patterns were learned by his mother's father. Unfortunately, my father continued to bring forth the lower energy of creation and repeated the same behavior patterns, because that's all he knew. At some point, each person must decide to seek a new and healthier vision of self to adopt as part of their own being, in order to break family cycles. You must look for the highest energy of your actions to choose from in order to obtain alignment in love. It is not always easy, but you have to try to choose love in all ways. Pure love never hurts!

My father was the first man in my life, and he came from a family who shaped him to become the man he was. However, my dad was the first man in my life who helped create the perception about all the other men in my life. This perception created a voice in me that used to say what I wanted in a man and what I did not want in a man. In the end, my father died while at someone's funeral, when he was giving a speech. He died penniless, and his last words were, "Love your family." But prior to his death, he came to me in a dream, and his spirit came to me on the day he died, before I received that dreadful call. As I look back, everything he was is what I needed to be who I am today.

Our Power

This power lives in every human being, and all I can assume is that a long time ago, this knowledge was kept away from various groups of people for whatever reason. However, God knew the plan. Look at us today; we are so blessed and have managed to accomplish so many things. We are given free will to accept or decline a diagnosis as true, and we have the power to heal with our minds. Whatever you give your attention to or believe to be true is up to *you* and not the world.

It is our free will to accept physical reality or to accept spiritual reality over what the eyes and ears witness day to day. Here is an example of this: My ex-boyfriend (the gentleman) was diagnosed with multiple sclerosis prior to our first meeting. I explained it to him this way—being in an agreement with what you heard can only have power on your body if you accept this diagnosis as your reality. The diagnosis can only be in your experience if you consent to having the disease. It is not the doctor who has the final say, but it is up to you. Today, as I write these words, he is no longer on medication or symptomatic of MS, and the doctors claim he must have been misdiagnosed.

I know now that this infinite energy will always choose love for you and me. However, our free will thinks of the worst-case versus the best-case scenario. Before realizing my power, I learned I had to let go of all the chatter. I learned I had to clear out the old chatter in my mind and to stop thinking of the worst thing that could happen and focus on the best outcome. I learned how to do transcendental meditation to help recover from my trauma. Through meditation, I have been able to quiet my mind more and become calmer and more clear-thinking. At first, I was skeptical, but I am not the only healer. I just did not know I was born to be a healer.

My Purpose!

Yes, it is time for solutions. So, I am here to do my part, my purpose, and explain why I was created. Why is this important? Because my dad should be alive, and my mom and siblings deserve the truth and the best life, not the one they have been living. Although my family was terribly affected, I want us all to have a life we were created to live because the universe/God loves us more than what I was taught from some of the churches that I attended throughout my life. I must be honest!

The universe really, really, really loves us! I learned that it is our own minds that do not love or believe in our spirit.

Who Should Be Reading This?

Unfortunately, those who need to read this book will not. Why? If you were raised like I was growing up, I was taught not to ask questions. I was trained in church to not question God, instead, to fear God and to only read the King James Version of the Bible, and when hearing a different perspective, reject it.

Well, that is not in my religion. How sad that some are one sneeze away from the grave and one dollar away from being on the streets or performing sexual favors for cash. I must tell you the truth!

Today, I understand that those fear-based thoughts caused me, my family, and so many others so much pain. We were taught in *fear*, which is the lowest energy of this universe. Fear is the worst emotion to carry in your thoughts and is responsible for creating your list of *I do not want* in the Spirit, which creates that fear-based thought into your physical reality.

Now, the question is, how can this book change my life? The answer is simple: if you are ready to **live your best life** and are **willing to learn**, I will provide you with real-life techniques I used to change my thinking. The first thing you must understand is that every day of your life is an accumulation of your past and present thoughts, played out in physical form. Let me say that another way. You are who you are today because of, and in spite of, everything that has happened to you up until now. When you understand that, you understand what I am about to say. My thoughts became things based on my accumulated journey. The instances I share with you will confirm this fact.

Everything you have experienced was soaked up by your subconscious mind. The subconscious mind is your inner spirit that never sleeps. The subconscious mind works even when you are sleeping, continually processing and soaking up everything you hear and see, whether you are asleep or awake. Think of your subconscious as a mini-megacomputer, taking everything in. So, for those who enjoy falling asleep to the TV, I would like to remind you that your mind is being programmed at that moment, and whatever you are hearing can become your life experience. You will be sitting somewhere, asking yourself, *What is happening to my life?* Your subconscious never stops. Now you can understand why a few days on the shoreline in Hawaii makes you feel so good. It's not just that you are there and having fun; it's that you are taking in the energy. If you do that for a week or so, you will begin to feel, well, *energized!*

Unlikely Messenger and Connector

We all have had our share of religious beliefs. I grew up in a holiness-sanctified church and was always told to only read the King James Version of the Bible and nothing else. All my life, I was taught to thank God in advance, be careful with the words I speak, and treat people the way I wanted to be treated. Truth be told, I did not always follow this knowledge. I tried, but it just did not happen that way. I believe one reason why I didn't follow the rules was because I thought I could simply get away with doing stupid stuff that I did not know was stupid in the first place. I confess to you, I was and still not perfect as the Church claimed I had to be. Believe it or not, I have a lot of love in me, but my fear left me desperate enough to do desperate things; my intentions were never to hurt anyone. I was locked in a world where I didn't know any other way to get what I wanted or needed.

However, I managed to attract the one of the wealthiest royal men from Nigeria, and I truly had a *Coming to America* love story. My Nigerian prince arrived in 2006, when I found myself alone with my daughters while living in Virginia, working the night shift and attending nursing school during the day.

It seemed the moment I stopped looking and decided that *no man* was my best option, this man appeared. He spoiled me and my daughters, and he would arrange for me to fly to wherever he was. He paid for a place for me and my girls to stay and bought me a laptop on our first date so I could email him. After months of dating, he found the home he wanted to buy me to be closer to one of his oil refineries in Texas. My prince asked me to have his child for his father to accept me and for us to be able to marry, due to my not being part of royalty. Unfortunately, months later, I became aware of him disappearing for periods of time. Then I found out he was married and could have three wives. What I know now is that I attracted the love I wanted to experience from watching *Coming to America* multiple times because it was my ex's favorite movie. Having been the other woman and a mistress was my fear because of who my dad was. I attracted those who were like my father, and I acted in accordance with my deepest fears.

My life continued to get better as I healed. I learned that at each painful moment in my life, I was acting on fear, and with each step closer, I was challenged by the obstacles and became stronger, wiser, and more enlightened. I knew that for me the work had to start with retraining my brain to begin healing from the beliefs, hurt, and fear I saw as a child and later experienced in my adulthood.

Pain = Prayer

Today I ask the questions I was supposed to ask God, but this time I do it without fear, like when I asked God the questions that I wanted answered. Today God, universe, or whatever you choose to call the Creator brings people into being with all the answers. The more I witnessed God's presence in my life, the more my faith grew. Before I reached consciousness or Christ conscious, I was clueless in knowing how the Spirit communicated with me. I always thought it was through a prophet at church or a psychic. However, I got answers after I asked, "Why am I here? Why did You create me? Why is there so much suffering? Why is my life this way?" I also felt something was not right, because my own thoughts made me feel bad, sad, uneasy, mad, and a full array of other forms of emotional pain.

God did answer all those questions in 2011, but the transformation wasn't overnight. It was seven years and three months later. So *do not* give up! I learned the hard way to hear God speak. All these years, I was waiting for a man's voice to talk to me. That was foolish. I understand now the voice is an inner voice that is always loving and without ego. I also learned that no two people have the same mind and desires. Even now when I ask God for a sign, I learn that I am on the right path; I get little hints.

Reason to Keep Going

I can relate to the same hell some of you are currently living in or revisiting each day. I understand why you may think you just can't seem to get a break, no matter what you have done or continue to do. It seems no matter how hard you have tried, there continues to be some sort of entrapment. I wanted to take my own life and simply die because I could not get a break; I just became so tired, and my heart became so heavy. I was lost and did not see any other way out until the day I wrote that suicide letter and the most unselfish question came into my mind: "If I take my life, who would take care of my children?" At that moment, I stopped typing, changed my heart and mind, and decided to surrender my problems and find joy in my journey. Really, it was that simple. I replaced my past thoughts of sadness, hopelessness, and worthlessness with my present feelings of joy and appreciation. I started having a better prayer life and knew it was really time to move on.

Before I wrote this book, I did not know that there was something more for me around the corner, but I had faith and hope that there was more. That something was grace and a plan for my life that was already created. My job was to use my free will to either make choices out of fear or out of love in finding my purpose. I get this now more than ever; I discovered that I was unconsciously co-creating with God all my life. The life I wanted was gradually being built in my imagination from the time I was a child and started experiencing so much pain. The worse the pain, the bigger the blessing because of the powerful prayer that was invoked.

Face Fear!

The majority of my desires from my heart came after taking a leap of faith to do what was necessary for my life. I had to learn to have faith in myself and believe in my vision to live in peace and provide for my daughters and me. I had to leave my relationship after twenty years of being together. I wanted peace and joy in my life, and it took me years to understand why it was never going to happen with the man I was with, as long as he fed me my fears.

Vision!

My unconscious thinking created a vision to move to Florida, work as a clinical research coordinator or clinical research associate, and start a life with my two daughters. I wanted to be able to attend NFL and NBA games, travel the world, attend any concert or event I desire, and have a life partner to do all of it with. He would be someone to celebrate my birthdays with, a man who would talk to me and spend time with me. He had to be African American, because I was over that royalty stuff. I also envisioned having chickens in my backyard and an avocado tree.

The move to Florida was not easy, but I was determined. The relocation was scary, so I went to therapy prior to my move. I had never lived in Florida and had only visited the state twice. When I made the move, I had about fourteen hundred dollars to my name and had just received that money the day I booked my ride on the Amtrak Auto-Train from Virginia to some town outside of Orlando, Florida. The money I received came from my first paycheck from a position I just got after being unemployed for almost three years. I also raised money for the move by turning my dining room into a store. I sold the majority of my clothes, handbags, and shoes, everything between one dollar and five dollars, which gave me an extra $150. I left that morning with the majority of my clothes in my car. Days earlier, I realized that I could not help my ex, and what I did not want him to know was that I always thought he was better than me, I wanted him to just be nice to me and make me feel beautiful. I simply wanted to be good enough for someone.

Thoughts Became Things

After fifteen years of nonstop studying to pursue a four-year college education, I finally obtained my bachelor's degree. I was in college from 1997 until 2012, determined to accomplish my only goal in life by taking one or two classes a semester as needed. In July 2012, after graduating, I asked the Lord to bless me with a clinical research coordinator or clinical research associate position. In August 2012, a recruiter called me for a position I never applied for or even considered. The position was a clinical research coordinator at a large cancer center. I know now that Spirit blessed me with a temporary position while living in Maryland and blessed me with the money I needed for a one-way ticket on the train, leaving me with enough gas money until I received my first paycheck from my new position.

Twin Soul Flame

In November 2013, I recall being sad on Thanksgiving while I was living in Florida and preparing for my children's arrival. I truly felt all alone. My mother suggested I go see a movie, and so I did. I didn't want to go alone, so I asked a friend of a friend to go with me. When I met this gentleman, everything seemed so familiar. I later found out we were both born on June 24, and his younger brother and my youngest daughter's birthdays were on December 28. He was also the CEO of a ticket brokerage company and had access to tickets to all the concerts and all the sporting events in Florida and other states and even countries.

I later realized while I was married that all of the tears I cried and prayers of asking God to bless me with a better relationship with a man who was like me, and there he was: an African American man who loves to travel and was college educated became my best friend. This man turned out to be everything I asked for and came into my life without me really looking for him.

We started dating, and before long, my daughters and I moved into his home. He had chickens in his backyard, and an avocado tree that was over fifty years old. After I realized that he was who I prayed for and that my life became a mirror of my journal, I asked my boyfriend, "How is it possible that everything I wrote about came true?" My twin flame later gave me two books to read. The first book was called *Conversations with God* by Neal Donald Walsch, and the second was *The Secret* by Rhonda Byrnes.

After reading these two books, I realized I was taught a lie, but not on purpose. I also discovered that I had been manifesting things and people all my life but was unconscious of the power that God put in me. I discovered that my journey created by God to be true, and what I studied for years and continue to seek for better understanding of what I encountered, I somehow managed to receive answers and guidance when the pain became enough to want a change.

Most often the change was to feel and give love. Some will say I am blessed, some will say I have favor over my life, and some will say I am lucky. However, I say I am profoundly grateful to God for showing me that love is always with me. I have to know I am loved at all times and I should never react with fear again. We all are one; we all are of the same spirit. What we do to another person we do to ourselves. When we live our lives this way, we are never punished, and we are pushing forward the positive flow of energy. I am whatever I believe because I now know God is in me every day, with each step I take.

Preconditioned into Lack and Limitations, Sickness, Greed, Fear, and Self-Hatred

So many of us want a change. When you think about a change in your life, are you willing to do the work, or will you take a back seat and continue to coexist? Can you accept that your life is what it is today due to the culmination of all your past personal perceptions of how you see yourself, the world, and circumstances? Can you accept the concept that your imagination truly, honestly, and lovingly creates your outer world? Can you accept the fact that your own fear creates bad circumstances in your life? Can you accept the belief that faith and love create greater circumstances in your life? No one asked me these questions when I was growing up! No one informed me that as I was living, I was creating my life through my emotions and not through my heart. Who would have thought this?

No one told me that I was intentionally created to create. No one informed me that I would become what I thought about, whether it was thoughts about me or others. No one advised me that what I did to others I was actually literally doing to myself. No one told me that I had power and could have anything I wanted in this life. So, my question to you is, what do you truly want to experience in every aspect of your life?

I have discovered that some questions you ask yourself are energy blockers. I have seen it play out in my life and in my family.

Are you quick to anger? Do your angry emotions feel good to you in any way? I was raised with that anger most of the time; every now and then, there were bits and pieces of sunshine. Anger can affect an entire city. I can attest to two states: Indiana and Michigan. These two states are the most low-energy places I have experienced. I often wonder, how can an entire city be blind to what is really going on there?

Growing up, I experienced horror and pain from so many friends being shot down in the streets. I watched most of the young men I grew up with end up in prison, trying to be about that life I had been observing but not consciously creating. What they do not know is that in order to do better, you have to see it and believe positive changes can take place in anyone's life.

Another thing I noticed is the anger in the hearts of so many who have constantly been touched by the negative side of life and are blind to why they ended up in bad situations and circumstances. Something as simple as looking at someone wrong is enough for them to want to fight you. They are ready to rip your head off because they convinced themselves through their own observations of others that they were being disrespected. This self-imposed projection happens with women providing sex for cash and men who enroll in this process, parents who are caught up in their dysfunction and not able to show up for their kids' PTA meetings or school activities, beatings like the plantation days, the child who angers because he or she can't read, and that child uses anger when asked to read out loud.

I personally encountered so much craziness growing up and into adulthood. I am sure you have seen the craziness in your life.

I was trying to figure out how the hell I could get out of that stuff in order to have a better life outside of the limited vision I had. I had asked myself the same questions for many years: Why was this my beginning? Why am I here, God? Why, God? Why did You create my family and me to suffer? Why does it seem like good things happen to people who don't have a heart like me?

It seemed that no matter what, I just could not get ahead. Knowing what I now know and becoming aware of that basic thought regarding not getting ahead actually started with my family. In other words, the blind were leading the blind down the same journey that led to nowhere. Words we hear and speak each day unconsciously become a part of our mind-set and have created the reality each of us is in today. I believe what sustained me were my constant thoughts and feelings that deep inside I just knew my family and I deserved more than what life was presenting to us. I knew deep inside as a little girl that we deserved love, joy, peace, prosperity, and abundance. What I didn't know was that my preacher at church contradicted what I knew in my spirit. I remember singing songs and praising God about not being worthy. OMG! I was so blind, and so was my church. Now, after putting myself in my own clinical trial and applying the skills I have learned as a clinical research professional and documenting the contrast, as I call it, (some would say the devil), I found something amazing. I found the power that comes out of each experience, and from this power I discovered the power of intentions.

The Trials

I t was not easy, but I knew in order to help my family, I had to separate from them and become the woman I saw in my vision. I left behind everything that tied me to my roots in Indiana and later discovered the truth about life and the power that we were born with. I discovered fear was the devil, and yes, it is in the mind, and yes, I wanted to be free.

I discovered the words I read, heard, spoke, and unconsciously heard from others' conversations, television, radio, and any words, for that matter, were creating my life every day. I discovered what I thought about me secretly became my reality, no matter what. I discovered I was always worthy and unlike what I shouted out all the time in church as a child: the words, "I am not worthy, but you love me Lord" and a song called, "If I Suffer, I Will Get Eternal Life," two things that are often repeated over and over in Black churches. I am only speaking the truth.

Unfortunately, these people continue to suffer and have no idea it is their praise, and yes, it used to be mine. I tell you one thing: when you know better, you should try something new just to see if you will get different results. I decided to do something different and learn something I didn't know. Unfortunately, so many religious people are afraid to read another book outside of the Bible for direction and clarity, as if God stopped working through people. I was raised not to read anything else besides the Bible and to never question God. However, the inner guide in me knew better; I knew something was missing, and I began to follow the voice inside of me. I discovered we all can live and love the way we see it and believe it, and it doesn't matter what your religion is.

You are What You Think About

I t is very true, and it is my testimony: whether you are thinking about yourself or someone else, it will show up in your life. We are constantly creating situations and events in our own lives without any exceptions to the rules, through our imagination and thoughts. When I first discovered this for myself, it was crazy for me.

I remember asking myself, God loves me *that* much? I began to cry because I just couldn't believe I was that free. Was it true that all I had to do was think positive and loving thoughts to create a new life and circumstances for me and put action into what I wanted? Well, I began believing that it could be done, and maybe it would be easy to do.

I grew up in a home where people were broken, mentally and spiritually. I had this hunger and wanted to break free. I knew mental slavery started in the mind, so the healing had to start there as well, and I did my work.

I am speaking to every nation and race and country. Every individual. If you are living in poverty and have a lack of food, shelter, and clothes, this book is for you. If you are chopping up people for their body parts for magical potions or discriminating against anyone, this book is for you. Yes, many were broken many years ago and passed on the seed of lack. Truth is, the lack is only there because you believe it's there, in your mind. You have no idea the work it took for me to figure out how to change something when I physically saw the problem. But in order to have more of what you want, you have to believe it subconsciously. I want to assist you in waking up. It does not matter if your street is stricken with gang members, prostitution, drug dealers, drug addicts, murderers, religious groups saying you are not worthy, living in the ghetto, on a public housing voucher, or locked in prison. Change the way you think, and pretend like a child.

You Can Live Your Life the Way You See It in Your Imagination

I write this to say that *life* is what you decide it to be after you wake up from false beliefs you were born into. Your task is to retrain your brain so that no one is a threat or can compete for what is your birthright to have. I actually did this. Change is truly not easy, especially when breaking a negative mind-set, but it can be done.

I understand that in all of us, our beginning was never our choice, but after you leave your childhood home, the outcome of your life truly depends on you and you alone. If you grew up in a dysfunctional family, you have two choices. You can use what hurt you to grow and love beyond, or you can allow what hurt you to enter your mind and continue to play out in your life. No matter what happened then, what you want now is in your present moment. It is clearly up to you. The key thing I realized was that in order to change my life, I had to change my perception of my family and community. It taught me through words, actions, routines, rituals and all things that I could see, hear, touch, smell, and taste. All of it, wrapped up into the mold of me, including the constant thought about the lack of money and other resources. It took me years to understand the saying, "The poor keep getting poorer, and the rich keep getting richer." Because each person is living out their beliefs.

When I realized what the heck was going on, I decided to study and watch those who had money and those who did not. I realized and discovered that both positions were a state of mind. You have heard this before: whatever a man or woman thinks he or she is, so be it! This may sound fairytale-like, but it is very true. You will have exactly what you say you want!

I actually tested my theory out, and it became very clear to me that **like attracts like.** During this discovery, I was moved to tears. I just did not know all this time why I kept getting what I was getting. I decided to forget whatever I knew and learn from my family and change my thinking. The only thought I held on to was what my grandmother taught me, and that was my faith, gratitude, and not believing in negative words from others. She taught me to ignore negativity, and my mother taught me to take those negative words and use them as fuel to motivate myself to accomplish my goals.

So, all of this sounds really good, but I discovered a problem trying to implement this theory: first I had to feel good. I could not find one book that was able to answer my simple question, *How can someone feel good when he or she does not physically see the money and is having trouble buying food and providing shelter or is homeless or abused? How can you feel good when you are in the midst of your storm?*

The thing is, in order to change anything, it starts in the mind, period. Remember, this is why you are in your situation in the first place. When we worry, we create more worry; there is no faith in worry. I didn't want to admit it, but it was true. I learned through my journey that on the day after I was going to take my life, things shifted. Why? Because I told myself that I was going to stand on faith once and for all and enjoy the journey—gratitude and faith! I had nothing else to lose, but I knew in my soul that I couldn't leave my children behind. Even through the tears that left me on my knees, screaming and begging God to save me and help me, it wasn't until I became grateful for what I had and became faith-filled that it fueled my imagination to turn things around. I can say proudly that I passed that test. So, if you have one crumb today, please feel the gratitude for it and ask in appreciation for more of what you need and know is yours when you asked the first time.

I realized years ago that I was more than I knew, and love is the only way. Some have told me that I am a seer, an angel of faith, and a prophet, especially during my teen years. To me, I am just Queen Buffy. I have been this way all my life and thought I was cursed to love people. No matter what, I can love anyone who would hurt me and intentionally hurt others. I literally stood in front of bullets to protect people I did not know and would stand up to guys that I saw beating up their girlfriends. I realize I simply had the courage to love just like Jesus, Buddha, Martin Luther King, and so many countless others over the years.

I have always had this love in me, and despite my upbringing, the love in me grew stronger, and so did my compassion for all mankind. This is why I wanted to write this book to the world, to reinforce what so many have been marching for, writing about, and announcing for years.

My fellow brothers and sisters, love and gratitude are the keys to opening doors to the life you desire. You can't even fake it either. You really have to clean out the whispers of hate, resentment, jealousy, envy, vindictiveness, anger, and all things that hold you back from feeling good, especially when it comes to negative self-talk.

My grandmother always used to say, "Be careful with what you say with your mouth." Whenever anyone spoke bad news to us, she would always say, "Do not listen to that mess; they do not know what they are talking about." My grandmother would remind me that there was life and death in the tongue. Growing up, I did not know what the heck she was talking about, but today I truly understand. I understand this so much that I stopped watching TV, listening to certain music, talking to certain people, and have become more careful where I go, how I spend my time, and who I spend it with. I learned how to filter the words I hear, even when someone is speaking. If I do not believe it, I will reject it in a heartbeat and pray instantly in my spirit.

Believe that you and everyone born here were not put on this Earth to suffer! Get this out of your subconscious now and forever. You were meant to live a life of abundance and joy.

You must stop holding on to that fear-based thought in your mind that truly was meant to do what it has done for generations. This fear-based, thought-created barrier built a mental wall for you to fear knowledge from others. This fear-based thought did the same thing to me for years and almost cost me my life.

My purpose, which I believe is for all of us, is to assist in healing our Earth from things that have continued to cause so much hell. I believe our beginnings and journeys were especially created for us. I believe all the hell we have been through is to assist us to become stronger, wiser, and have the wisdom to assist in destroying genocide, racism, killing, abuse, theft, religious extremism, and other destructive behaviors. It seems so many have been hurt and destroyed in the name of religion, yet they ignore that inner voice to choose love.

Pay attention to how you feel. We were all called to lead, to love, and to heal, but we sit still and judge others who aren't doing anything to us. Being gay bothers you? Why? Oh, the Bible says so? What is so sad is that I have the kingdom of God in me, and it started in my mind. I understand those who are gay. As long as you live here on this Earth, it will be really hard to experience the kingdom of heaven (God's peace) (love and peace) messing around with all those who want to be holier than others. I wonder, how will the world change when humans start to accept the kingdom of God (kingdom of love)? It starts within your mind, and God is love. What if we just love and mind our own business?

Slaying Your Spiritual Vampires

More than likely, you will meet many people who operate on a lower frequency than you and are not aware of the laws of the universe. Some are aware and will intentionally try to manipulate your energy. I suggest you become familiar with these laws. However, when you meet these energy vampires, know that they came because of your own energy field in the first place.

When you meet them, you will know because your inner fears will be triggered. Please do not take anything personally, but be thankful because they are only revealing to you your own insecurities and what needs to be healed within you. They will also reveal to you the power you gave away.

If I were you, I would study more about being an empath and learn more about narcissistic personality disorder. I was raised by a narcissist and dated many others, but you can't change them without betraying, hurting yourself, or dying. Your job will be to get your power back and to become your true self, even if that means moving away from everyone, standing up for yourself, and facing the fear of getting into trouble for speaking your truth. You want freedom? Then you must face your fears head on and let go of what someone thinks of you. If you continue to carry the fear of what someone thinks of you, you will continue to attract people who will attack your character and work ethic, and will pick you apart and betray you. Your energy is everything, and cleaning it up starts within your spirit.

You do not have to tell anyone what you are doing. As you do your energy work and fall in love with yourself, be grateful for where you are.

In my journey, I faced ten of those vampires at the same time. They will vibrate out of your life as you vibrate higher within. If they are in your home, be still and analyze what you need, in order to get your power back and do it and live with the purest intentions. Speak to the Lord, who is the provider for all people, and ask for what you need and desire if you feel stuck. I did this, and everything I needed was waiting for me. It must be authentic. You must believe your own words.

Most importantly, forgive others, because they do not understand that everything they did to you was already done to them. If you are a woman who is married, has kids, and does not work, the same is true for you. I left multiple times with two kids, and God sent so much in return to assist me.

And just in case you believe this lie, man is not your provider. Change your thinking. **The universe/God/the Lord/Spirit is your provider, and you are connected to it!**

New Kingdom Within

Prior to entering a new kingdom and paradigm, I learned the following without knowing it was going to shift me into consciousness and manifest what I prayed for. During my journey, I decided to enjoy the ride and practiced what I am about to write each day.

I loved everyone. I enjoyed my life with my children, my cat, and my dog, and I enjoyed my journey when I was attending college. I attended church every Sunday. I danced all the time. When I was being verbally attacked, I stated who I was: "I am smart, I am someone, I am moving to Florida to start a new life, and I will have a new car." (I only said this once because it was said when I was crying. I did not do repetition because I did not know these were affirmations at the time.)

I always had a grateful heart because I grew up without much. I learned to think about the end result only. I learned not to think of the obstacles because my mind created all the obstacles in my past. I learned what I believed in my mind, including that illness would come true if you BELIEVE it will, from my grandmother when I was a little girl. I learned to meditate and take naps to quiet my mind more. I learned to be mindful of what I listened to, what I talked about, and what I watched on TV. I stopped watching the news in 2012. I learned that my imagination was God, and the way I felt was extremely important. Most importantly, I learned to forgive and let go of the past because it was all the total manifestation of what I used to believe about myself, others, and life.

Slayed My Demons

My life is good and far from perfect, but I am better than I used to be. However, at the age of forty-two, I face my own demons while crying, shaking, praying, and doing the best I can. My twin flame encounter shifted me into Christ consciousness. I can admit I loved this man more than anyone in the world. He was so much like me, as if I knew him all my life. He was my mirror, and our encounter was powerful together as we masterminded together, and a disaster in the end. My twin flame helped me see me for the first time and the energy I had to heal. He brought me everything I wanted, and he was everything I hated. Because of him, I am blessed. I believe in me more, I love myself more, I accept myself, I approve of myself, I am stronger, and I had the courage to slay the demons he mirrored to me, which were my demons as well.

- I slayed the disease to please: I honor myself first whether people like it or not.
- I slayed the belief that I was not enough: I am more than enough! I am everything!
- I slayed the belief that a man was my provider and protector: God is my provider and my protector.
- I slayed codependency: I fill up my own cup first and do what makes me happy.

- I slayed the belief of not being worthy: I am worthy of the very best!
- I slayed the belief of not being lovable: I am lovable!

Basically, love is the energy source, so do your best to love the life you live now. Focus on what you love, fall in love with yourself now, accept everything about yourself, and create something phenomenal from all the bad stuff by praying and asking for what you prefer.

Love yourself unconditionally, like your life depends on it—because it does. And do your best to love all people unconditionally.

—Queen Buffy

CPSIA information can be obtained
at www.ICGtesting.com
Printed in the USA
BVHW030559100321
602114BV00001B/166